ARMED FORCES

★ ★ ★

UNITED STATES

NAVY

by Jack David

TORQUE
TM

This edition first published in 2008 by Bellwether Media.

No part of this publication may be reproduced in whole
or in part without written permission of the publisher.
For information regarding permission, write to Bellwether
Media Inc., Attention: Permissions Department,
Post Office Box 19349, Minneapolis, MN 55419-0349.

Library of Congress
David, Jack, 1968–
  United States Navy / by Jack David.
     p. cm. — (Torque: Armed Forces)
  Includes bibliographical references and index.
  ISBN-13: 978-1-60014-165-2 (hbk. : alk. paper)
  ISBN-10: 1-60014-165-X (hbk. : alk. paper)
  1. United States. Navy—Juvenile literature. I. Title.
  VA58.4.D38 2008
  359.00973–dc22   2007042410

CONTENTS

★ ★ ★

★ ★ ★

Chapter One

WHAT IS THE UNITED STATES NAVY?

very day and night, ships of the United States Navy patrol the world's oceans. The Navy's goal is to protect the nation's shores and waterways. It uses its ships, aircraft, and other vehicles to fight battles from the sea. It also helps enforce international laws at sea. Ship captains and their crews work together to complete their **missions**.

The U.S. Navy is one of the branches of the **United States Armed Forces**. The other branches are the Air Force, Army, Coast Guard and Marine Corps. The five branches all work together to defend the country.

Chapter Two

VEHICLES, WEAPONS, AND TOOLS OF THE NAVY

The Navy has many important vehicles. Most are oceangoing. Some serve on land or in the air.

88

Nimitz-class supercarrier

Aircraft carriers are the Navy's largest ships. They are like floating airports. Planes and helicopters can take off from and land on their massive decks. The Nimitz-class supercarriers are the largest of all aircraft carriers. These are powered by **nuclear energy**.

The USS Harry S. Truman Nimitz-class supercarrier is 1,096 feet (334 meters) long. That's longer than three football fields!

Some ships are built for fighting. Destroyers and cruisers are built to protect the **fleet.** They're loaded with weapons. They fire guns and surface-to-air **missiles** at enemy planes. They launch underwater **torpedoes** at enemy ships.

Torpedo

The Ohio-class submarines are the largest submarines in service for the Navy. They are designed to stay at sea for months at a time. They are armed with powerful nuclear missiles called Tridents. For that reason, these submarines are known as the Trident submarines.

Submarines patrol under the ocean surface. They can stay underwater for weeks at a time. They use a tool called **sonar** to find their way in the dark depths of the ocean. Sonar equipment sends out sound waves. The waves bounce back when they hit solid objects such as other ships or the ocean floor.

Planes and helicopters are also important for the Navy. Fighter planes such as the F/A-18 Hornet patrol the skies. They can attack enemy planes or ships. Helicopters like the H-60 Seahawk series fight in battles, carry people and supplies, and help with water rescues. Planes and helicopters can take off from naval bases on land or from aircraft carriers on the water.

F/A-18 Super Hornet has a maximum speed of 1,190 miles (1,915 kilometers) per hour.

F/A-18 Hornet

All enlisted members of the U.S. Navy go through their basic training at the Great Lakes Training Center in Illinois.

Chapter Three

LIFE IN THE NAVY

Basic training

Every member of the U.S. Navy has an important role. Each person has a **rank**. Most people in the Navy are **enlisted members**. They start in **basic training**. They go through drills, classes, and tests. Then they train for special jobs. They may learn to operate weapons or fix engines. They may perform jobs on a ship. Sailors often serve on board a ship for months at a time. Other sailors serve on land at naval bases.

★ ★ ★ **19**

The highest rank in the Navy is admiral. Admirals make the most important decisions in the Navy.

Officers are in charge of the enlisted members. They must get leadership training. Some attend college at the U.S. Naval Academy in Maryland. All go to advanced training at the Navy Officer Candidate School (OCS) in Rhode Island. When they finish training, they are prepared for a leadership role in the United States Navy.

Officers

★ ★ ★

basic training—the course of drills, physical tests, and military training that new enlisted members of the U.S. Armed Forces must go through

enlisted member—a person in the U.S. Armed Forces who ranks below an officer; all enlisted members are currently volunteers.

fleet—a group of ships

missile—an explosive that can be launched at targets on the ground or in the air

mission—a military task

nuclear energy—energy produced from splitting atoms

officer—a member of the armed forces who ranks above enlisted members

rank—a specific position and level of responsibility in a group

sonar—a device used to detect objects underwater using sound waves

torpedo—an underwater missile

United States Armed Forces—the five branches of the U.S. military; they are the Air Force, the Army, the Coast Guard, the Marine Corps, and the Navy.

TO LEARN MORE

★ ★ ★

AT THE LIBRARY

Bartlett, Richard. *United States Navy*. Chicago, Ill.: Heinemann, 2004.

Braulick, Carrie A. *U.S. Navy Aircraft Carriers*. Mankato, Minn.: Capstone, 2006.

David, Jack. *United States Marine Corps*. Minneapolis, Minn.: Bellwether, 2008.

ON THE WEB

Learning more about the United States Navy is as easy as 1, 2, 3.

1. Go to www.factsurfer.com

2. Enter "Navy" into search box.

3. Click the "Surf" button and you will see a list of related web sites.

With factsurfer.com, finding more information is just a click away.

INDEX

★ ★ ★